From Archangel to Geometry: Metatron's Cube and Its Spiritual Legacy

M.A Hill

Published by M.A. Hill, 2024.

FROM ARCHANGEL TO GEOMETRY: METATRON'S CUBE AND ITS SPIRITUAL LEGACY

First edition. March 14, 2024.

ISBN: 979-8224368471

Written by M.A Hill.

'From Archangel to Geometry: Metatron's Cube and Its Spiritual Legacy'

Table of Contents

1 1. The Origins of Metatron's Cube

1 The Legend of Archangel Metatron
2 Ancient Symbols and Their Meanings

2 2. The Sacred Geometry of Metatron's Cube

3 3. Metatron's Cube in Various Spiritual Traditions

4 4. The Metaphysical Properties of Metatron's Cube

5. Symbolism and Esoteric Meanings of Metatron's Cube

1 Transformation and Evolution
  2 Connection to Higher Realms
  3 Guardian of Sacred Knowledge

6 6. Metatron's Cube and Ascension Consciousness

1 Activation of Light Body

2 Alignment with Cosmic Energies

3 Expansion of Conscious Awareness

7 7. Exploring Metatron's Cube in Modern Spirituality

8 8. Personal Growth and Metatron's Cube

1 Self-Discovery and Inner Wisdom

2 Transformational Tools

3 Finding Purpose and Clarity

9 9. Manifestation and Metatron's Cube

1 Power of Visualization
2 Quantum Reality
3 Law of Attraction

10 10. Metatron's Cube and Planetary Healing

1 Raising Vibrational Frequencies

2 Environmental Stewardship

3 Global Unity and Compassion

11 11. Mystical Experiences with Metatron's Cube

12 12. Therapeutic Applications of Metatron's Cube

1 Energy Medicine

    2 Chakra Alignment

    3 Harmonizing Mind, Body, and Spirit

13 13. Metatron's Cube in Art and Architecture

1 Sacred Artifacts   15

   2 Sacred Geometry in Design

   3 Architectural Significance and Influence

14 14. Metatron's Cube and Quantum Physics

15 15. The Future of Metatron's Cube

1. The Origins of Metatron's Cube

The Legend of Archangel Metatron

The Legend of Archangel Metatron

Archangel Metatron has captivated the minds and hearts of spiritual seekers for centuries. His legend traces back to ancient mystical traditions, where he is often depicted as a mighty angelic being with a profound connection to the divine realm. In various belief systems, Metatron is believed to have played a crucial role in the creation and preservation of the universe.

In Jewish mysticism, known as Kabbalah, it is said that Metatron was once a human prophet known as Enoch. According to legend, Enoch was so righteous and dedicated to his spiritual path that he ascended to the status of an angelic being, becoming Metatron. He was then given the sacred duty of serving as the intermediary between heaven and earth, transmitting divine messages and wisdom to humanity.

Metatron's significance extends beyond the boundaries of Judaism. He is also revered in Christian and New Age traditions, where he is associated with spiritual transformation, divine knowledge, and higher consciousness. In these belief systems, Metatron is regarded as one of the highest-ranking angels, often referred to as the scribe of God or the angel of life.

Metatron's Cube, a sacred symbol that encapsulates the teachings and energies associated with Archangel Metatron, is believed to hold immense spiritual power. It is a geometric pattern consisting of interconnected circles, lines, and shapes. Each element of this intricate symbol represents a different aspect of the universe and the divine wisdom embodied by the archangel.

Through the symbol of Metatron's Cube, seekers of spiritual truth are invited to explore the profound mysteries and spiritual insights that lie beyond the physical realm. It serves as a reminder of the interconnectedness of all things and the limitless potential for growth and transformation that exists within each individual.

As you delve deeper into the legend of Archangel Metatron and the symbolism of Metatron's Cube, you are bound to encounter a wealth of spiritual teachings and metaphysical insights. The journey towards understanding the significance of this divine being and his sacred symbol is one that requires an open mind, a sense of reverence, and a genuine curiosity for the unknown.

In the following sections, we will explore the divine role and attributes associated with Archangel Metatron in various belief systems. Through this exploration, we will gain a deeper understanding of the profound impact that Metatron has had on the spiritual journeys of countless individuals throughout history.

Ancient Symbols and Their Meanings

Ancient Symbols and Their Meanings

Discover the captivating world of ancient symbols and unlock the profound wisdom they hold. Throughout history, humans have used symbols to convey complex ideas and spiritual truths. These symbols, rooted in various cultures and belief systems, have become timeless representations of deep spiritual insights.

One such symbol that encapsulates a multitude of spiritual insights is Metatron's Cube. This sacred symbol is named after the archangel Metatron and has been revered by numerous spiritual traditions around the world.

Metatron's Cube is a complex geometric pattern that consists of thirteen circles connected by straight lines. Each circle represents a profound aspect of the universe, and the connections between them symbolize the interdependence and interconnectedness of all things.

One can approach the interpretation of Metatron's Cube with a reverence for the ancient wisdom it embodies. The symbol invites us to contemplate the unity and harmony that underlies the universe. Its intricate design serves as a visual representation of the divine order that permeates all existence.

When exploring the meaning of Metatron's Cube, curiosity becomes an invaluable companion. Allow yourself to dive deep into the mysteries concealed within the symbol's intricate patterns. Each circle and line holds a profound spiritual message, waiting to be unveiled.

Openness is key when engaging with the esoteric wisdom encoded within Metatron's Cube. Approach this ancient symbol with an open mind and heart, ready to receive its insights. Allow the symbol to guide you on a transformative journey, leading to self-discovery and personal growth.

2. The Sacred Geometry of Metatron's Cube

The Platonic Solids

The Platonic Solids hold a special place in the realms of spirituality, metaphysics, symbolism, and personal growth. These five iconic geometric shapes, known as the Tetrahedron, Cube, Octahedron, Dodecahedron, and Icosahedron, have captivated the human imagination for centuries. Within their elegant simplicity lies a profound wisdom that transcends time and culture.

Each Platonic Solid is defined by several unique attributes. The Tetrahedron, for example, consists of four equilateral triangles, representing the element of fire and the sacred number three. The Cube, with its six square faces, embodies the stability and grounding energy of the earth.

The Octahedron, formed by eight equilateral triangles, symbolizes the harmonious relationship between the elements of air and water. The Dodecahedron, composed of twelve pentagons, represents the universe and the celestial realms. Lastly, the Icosahedron, comprised of twenty equilateral triangles, embodies the fluidity and adaptability of the water element.

These Platonic Solids are not just mere mathematical concepts; they hold deep spiritual significance. Exploring their symbolism and understanding their relationship to the mysteries of the universe can lead to profound personal insights and transformative experiences.

Metatron's Cube is a sacred geometric symbol that is intricately connected to the Platonic Solids. It is named after the angel Metatron, known as the scribe of God, believed to hold the keys to divine knowledge and sacred geometry.

Metatron's Cube consists of all the Platonic Solids nested within it, creating an exquisite web of interconnectedness. It is a visual representation of the divine order and the underlying structure of the cosmos.

By exploring the geometric patterns within Metatron's Cube, we gain insights into the fundamental principles of creation and the interconnectedness of all things. The geometric shapes within the cube are not just symbols; they are portals to higher realms of consciousness and spiritual understanding.

Unlocking the secrets of Metatron's Cube enables us to tap into its profound energies and align ourselves with the divine blueprint of existence. It helps us create a harmonious balance between our physical, mental, and spiritual aspects, allowing us to experience a deeper sense of purpose and connection with the universe.

Fibonacci Sequence and Divine Proportion

The Fibonacci Sequence and the Divine Proportion have long been recognized as potent symbols of divine harmony and mathematical beauty. Within the intricate patterns of Metatron's Cube, we find a convergence of these mathematical principles, presenting us with a gateway to explore the profound mysteries of our existence.

The Fibonacci Sequence, named after the Italian mathematician Leonardo Fibonacci, is a sequence of numbers where each number is the sum of the two preceding numbers (e.g., 0, 1, 1, 2, 3, 5, 8, 13, 21, and so on). This sequence appears abundantly in nature, from the branching of trees to the spirals of seashells. Its presence in the natural world reflects the underlying order and interconnectedness that permeates all aspects of creation.

The Divine Proportion, also known as the Golden Ratio or Phi (Φ), is a mathematical ratio that can be found in various natural and man-made forms. It is approximately equal to 1.61803398875. This ratio exudes an aesthetic appeal and is often associated with beauty, balance, and harmony. It has been celebrated throughout history by artists, architects, and philosophers as a symbol of divine perfection.

In the context of Metatron's Cube, the Fibonacci Sequence and the Divine Proportion take on a new level of significance. As we explore the intricacies of this sacred symbol, we are invited to contemplate the inherent beauty and symmetry that emerge from the mathematical principles underlying its design.

Metatron's Cube is composed of thirteen circles, each representing one of the thirteen spheres of the Tree of Life in the Kabbalah. The intricate geometric patterns formed by these circles are not only visually stunning but also hold deep spiritual meaning. They serve as a powerful tool for contemplation and meditation, allowing us to connect with the divine energies that flow through us and the universe.

As we delve into the symbolism of Metatron's Cube, we awaken a sense of reverence, curiosity, and openness to the profound mysteries and spiritual insights encapsulated within this symbol. Each line, shape, and proportion within its design carries a hidden message, guiding us towards a deeper understanding of ourselves and our place in the cosmos.

Fractal Nature of Metatron's Cube

Dive into a world where mathematics and spirituality converge, revealing a profound understanding of the universe and our place within it. Metatron's Cube is a symbol laden with meaning and mystery, capturing our imagination and sparking a sense of curiosity and wonder. In this subchapter, we will delve into the fractal nature of Metatron's Cube, unraveling its secrets and uncovering the profound insights it holds.

Metatron's Cube is a geometric figure that consists of interconnected spheres or circles, forming a complex pattern of lines and shapes. It is named after the archangel Metatron, who is said to hold the knowledge of the universe and act as a bridge between the divine and the earthly realms. This symbol has been revered throughout history for its symmetrical beauty and spiritual significance.

One of the key elements of Metatron's Cube is its fractal nature. Fractals are infinitely complex patterns that repeat themselves at different scales, creating a sense of infinite intricacy and self-similarity. As we study Metatron's Cube, we begin to see the fractal patterns emerge, revealing the interconnectedness of the microcosm and the macrocosm. It is through the exploration of fractal geometry that we gain a deeper understanding of the hidden order and harmony underlying the universe.

Fractals can be found everywhere in nature, from the branching of trees to the formation of snowflakes. They are expressions of the underlying mathematical principles that govern the universe. By studying these fractal patterns, we can unlock insights into the fundamental laws that shape our reality and tap into the spiritual wisdom embedded within.

Metatron's Cube serves as a portal to this hidden realm of fractal geometry. By contemplating its intricate patterns and exploring its mathematical foundations, we open ourselves up to new perspectives and profound revelations. It invites us to expand our consciousness and embrace the interconnectedness of all things. Metatron's Cube reminds us that we are part of a greater whole, connected to the fabric of the cosmos itself. Through this understanding, we can find deeper meaning in our lives and embark on a journey of personal growth and spiritual transformation.

3. Metatron's Cube in Various Spiritual Traditions

Kabbalistic Interpretations

The esoteric teachings and mystical interpretations of Metatron's Cube within the Kabbalistic tradition hold a captivating allure for those on a spiritual path. It is a symbol that encapsulates profound mysteries and spiritual insights, inviting us to delve deeper into the realms of symbolism, metaphysics, and personal growth.

As we explore the significance of Metatron's Cube in facilitating spiritual ascension and inner transformation according to Kabbalistic teachings, we are embarking on a journey of curiosity and openness. Let us embark on this exploration with a sense of reverence, recognizing the profound wisdom that Metatron's Cube holds.

Metatron in Christianity and Islam

Metatron holds a significant role in both Christian and Islamic traditions. Known as the angel of the presence, Metatron is believed to be an intermediary between humans and the divine. One of the most intriguing symbols associated with Metatron is Metatron's Cube, a sacred geometric pattern that represents the interconnectedness of the universe and the divine.

In Christianity, Metatron's role is believed to be that of a heavenly scribe. He is said to keep a record of all the deeds and actions of humanity, serving as a spiritual guide and advisor. In Islamic traditions, Metatron, known as Mīṭaṭrūsh, is also considered to be a guardian angel who plays a pivotal role in the heavenly realm.

Now let us delve deeper into the parallels and divergences found in the interpretations of Metatron and Metatron's Cube in these two monotheistic religions.

In Christianity, Metatron is often associated with Enoch, a figure from the Old Testament who was said to have walked with God and was taken up to heaven. It is believed that he was transformed into the angel Metatron, tasked with recording the divine secrets and serving as a divine emissary. Metatron is revered as a teacher and guide, offering wisdom and knowledge to those who seek a closer connection with the divine.

In Islamic traditions, Metatron, known as Mīṭaṭrūsh, is considered to be an angel who stands in the presence of Allah. Like in Christianity, Metatron is believed to be a guide and protector, assisting believers in their spiritual journey and providing insight into the divine mysteries. The significance of Metatron in Islam is linked to the teachings of the Prophet Muhammad, where he is mentioned as one of the highest-ranking angels.

Metatron's Cube holds great spiritual significance in both Christian and Islamic traditions. This sacred geometric pattern is composed of thirteen circles, representing the thirteen archangels, with Metatron at the center. The interlocking lines form a three-dimensional shape known as a cube, symbolizing the interconnectedness of all things in the universe.

Metatron's Cube is believed to hold profound spiritual insights and mysteries. It represents the harmony and balance between the physical and spiritual realms, reminding us of the divine order that underlies everything in creation. Through contemplation and meditation on Metatron's Cube, individuals can gain a deeper understanding of their place in the universe and the interconnectedness of all beings.

By exploring the role of Metatron and the symbolism of Metatron's Cube in Christian and Islamic traditions, we open ourselves to the profound mysteries and spiritual insights encapsulated within this symbol. With reverence, curiosity, and openness, we embark on a journey of personal growth and spiritual awakening, connecting with the divine and uncovering the deeper truths of existence.

Eastern Philosophies and Metatron's Cube

Metatron's Cube is a symbol that has deep connections with various Eastern philosophies, including Hinduism and Buddhism. In this subchapter, we will explore the intriguing intersection of these Eastern spiritual traditions with the profound symbolism of Metatron's Cube. Prepare to embark on a fascinating journey that will uncover spiritual insights and transformative practices associated with this sacred symbol.

4. The Metaphysical Properties of Metatron's Cube

Healing and Balance

Metatron's Cube is a symbol that holds immense power and significance in the realm of spirituality, metaphysics, and personal growth. It is believed to possess healing potential and the ability to restore harmony on physical, emotional, and spiritual levels. Let us delve into the mysteries and insights encapsulated within this sacred symbol.

At its core, Metatron's Cube is a geometric pattern that consists of interconnected circles, forming a unique and intricate design. This sacred symbol is named after Archangel Metatron, who is often associated with divine insights, spiritual guidance, and energetic balance. The exploration of Metatron's Cube allows us to tap into the profound energies it holds.

When we contemplate the healing potential of Metatron's Cube, we open ourselves up to a world of infinite possibilities. The interconnectedness of the circles within the symbol symbolizes the interconnectedness of all aspects of our being. It serves as a reminder that our physical, emotional, and spiritual dimensions are all intertwined, and the harmonious balance of these aspects is crucial for overall well-being.

By meditating on Metatron's Cube and visualizing its intricate pattern, we can invite energetic balance into our lives. This symbol serves as a gateway to connect with higher realms and tap into the divine wisdom that exists beyond our physical reality. Through this connection, we can gain insights, clarity, and a deeper understanding of our own spiritual journey.

The sacred geometry of Metatron's Cube has the power to stimulate and activate our energetic centers, also known as chakras. As we immerse ourselves in the symbol's energy, we can envision its intricate patterns aligning and balancing our chakras, thereby restoring harmony and promoting well-being.

Moreover, Metatron's Cube can be utilized as a tool for energetic cleansing and clearing. By visualizing the symbol around ourselves or others, we can release stagnant and negative energies, making way for the flow of positive, healing vibrations. The powerful energy of this symbol helps to dissolve blockages and restore the natural flow of life force energy within our energetic bodies.

In conclusion, Metatron's Cube holds tremendous healing potential and serves as a powerful tool for restoring harmony and promoting well-being on physical, emotional, and spiritual levels. When we approach this symbol with reverence, curiosity, and an open mind, we tap into its profound mysteries and unlock spiritual insights that can transform our lives. Let us embrace the energy of Metatron's Cube and embark on a journey of healing, balance, and self-discovery.

Meditative Practices

Discover the powerful meditative techniques that can be utilized with Metatron's Cube to access higher states of consciousness and inner stillness. This sacred symbol holds profound mysteries and spiritual insights that can greatly enhance your meditation practice. Let us embark on a journey of reverence, curiosity, and openness as we explore the transformative effects of Metatron's Cube meditation.

As you delve into the world of Metatron's Cube meditation, you will find a plethora of techniques to deepen your mindfulness and spiritual connection. Each practice is designed to awaken your sense of wonder and unlock the immense potential within yourself. Regardless of your background or beliefs, this subchapter will guide you on a path of self-discovery, growth, and spiritual awakening.

One of the primary techniques we will explore is known as Contemplating the Sacred Geometry. Metatron's Cube is a sacred geometric pattern that encompasses the building blocks of creation. By immersing yourself in the intricate symmetries and proportions of this symbol, you will enter a state of profound stillness and peace. Allow yourself to be captivated by the intricate interconnectedness that lies within Metatron's Cube.

Another technique we will delve into is called Breathwork and Visualization. Through conscious breathing and visualization exercises, you will learn to harness the energy and power of Metatron's Cube. This practice will enable you to connect deeply with the universal life force, expanding your awareness and consciousness.

Furthermore, we will explore the practice of Mantra Meditation. By chanting and repeating sacred sounds, you will tap into the vibrational frequencies and spiritual resonance of Metatron's Cube. This form of meditation has been practiced for centuries and is renowned for its ability to quiet the mind, open the heart, and align with the divine essence of the universe.

Lastly, we will delve into the practice of Energy Healing. Metatron's Cube serves as a potent tool for healing and balancing your energetic body. We will explore various techniques that utilize this sacred symbol to ground your energy, activate your chakras, and release any blockages or stagnant energy. Through these practices, you will experience a greater sense of harmony, vitality, and inner peace.

Open your heart, expand your consciousness, and embrace the mysteries and insights that Metatron's Cube holds. Join us on this transformative journey of self-discovery as we unlock the hidden depths of your spirituality, metaphysics, symbolism, and personal growth. Let the profound power of Metatron's Cube meditation guide you towards a more balanced, connected, and enlightened life.

Manifestation and Intention Setting

Manifestation and Intention Setting

Manifestation is the art of bringing your desires into reality through focused intention and alignment with the cosmic forces that govern our universe. Metatron's Cube is a powerful symbol that can assist us in this process, serving as a gateway to tap into divine energy and co-create our reality in accordance with the universal order.

When it comes to intention setting, Metatron's Cube offers a profound tool for aligning our thoughts, emotions, and actions with the highest vibrations of the cosmos. As we delve into the mysteries and spiritual insights encapsulated within this symbol, we open ourselves up to a world of infinite possibilities and potential.

One technique for utilizing Metatron's Cube in intention setting is to first connect with the energy of the symbol. Take a moment to observe its intricate patterns, allowing yourself to be drawn into its geometric perfection. Feel the reverence and curiosity welling up within you as you contemplate the sacred nature of this symbol.

As you harness the manifestation power of Metatron's Cube, take the time to clarify your intentions. What is it that you truly desire to manifest in your life? Whether it be abundance, love, healing, or spiritual growth, be clear and specific about your intentions.

Once your intentions are set, imagine yourself merging with the energy of Metatron's Cube. Visualize the symbol enveloping you, becoming a part of your being. As you do this, feel the cosmic forces flowing through you, aligning your thoughts and emotions with your desired outcome.

Next, use the symbol as a focal point for your intentions. Create a visual representation of your desires by placing the symbol in front of you or visualizing it in your mind's eye. See your intentions manifesting within the confines of the sacred geometry, knowing that the energy of Metatron's Cube is amplifying and magnifying your intentions.

As you work with Metatron's Cube, remember to remain open and receptive to the guidance and insights that may come. The symbol serves as a portal to higher realms of consciousness, opening the door to spiritual revelations and transformative experiences. Trust in the process and the wisdom that unfolds.

In conclusion, Metatron's Cube is a potent tool for manifestation and intention setting. By tapping into its powerful energy and aligning ourselves with cosmic forces, we can co-create our reality in alignment with divine order. Approach this practice with reverence, curiosity, and an open heart, and allow the profound mysteries and spiritual insights encapsulated within the symbol of Metatron's Cube to guide you on your journey of manifestation and personal growth.

5. Symbolism and Esoteric Meanings of Metatron's Cube

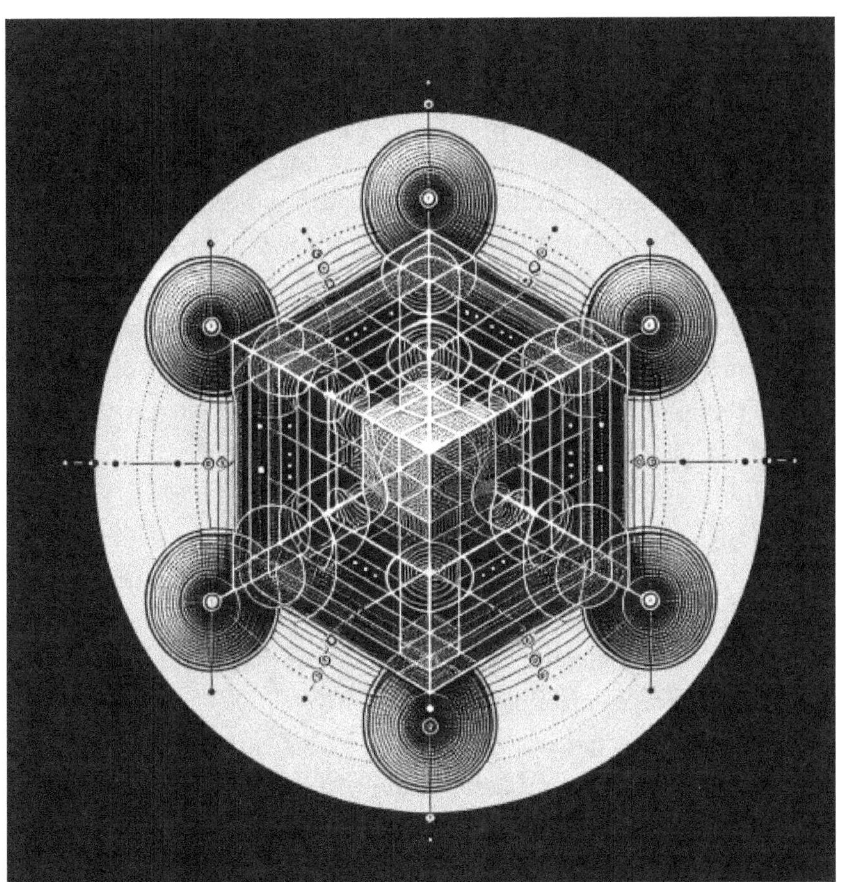

Transformation and Evolution

In the quest for spiritual growth and personal evolution, there are powerful symbols that serve as catalysts for transformation. One such symbol is Metatron's Cube, a geometric pattern that holds deep metaphysical significance. Delving into the transformative symbolism of Metatron's Cube can unlock profound insights and guide us on our journey towards self-realization.

Metatron's Cube represents the potential for transcendence, offering a gateway to expanded consciousness and higher realms of existence. Its intricate design consists of thirteen circles, each representing a different aspect of creation and divine energy. These circles are interconnected by lines, forming a complex web of interwoven patterns.

The symbolism contained within Metatron's Cube is multifaceted, inviting us to explore various layers of meaning and interpretation. At its core, this sacred symbol embodies the concept of unity and interconnectedness. It reminds us that we are all part of a larger cosmic tapestry and that everything in the universe is intricately interconnected.

The transformation and evolution subchapter elaborates on the transformative power of Metatron's Cube. It is an exploration of how this symbol can ignite personal growth and guide us towards self-discovery. Within the pages of this subchapter, we will delve into the profound mysteries and spiritual insights encapsulated within Metatron's Cube.

Through the lens of Metatron's Cube, we will examine the various aspects of our lives that are ripe for transformation. From our relationships and careers to our beliefs and perspectives, the symbol invites us to question and evolve. It reminds us that change is not only possible but necessary for spiritual growth.

This subchapter conveys a sense of reverence, curiosity, and openness to the profound mysteries that lie within Metatron's Cube. It encourages readers to approach the symbol with a receptive mindset, ready to explore its transformative power.

Whether you are a seasoned spiritual seeker or someone who is just beginning to explore the realms of metaphysics and symbolism, this subchapter will provide valuable insights and guidance. It is designed for a diverse audience united by a shared interest in spirituality, metaphysics, symbolism, and personal growth.

Connection to Higher Realms

Metatron's Cube, a sacred symbol with ancient origins, holds a profound connection to higher realms of consciousness and spiritual dimensions. This mystic symbol is known to unlock hidden knowledge and divine wisdom, inviting us to explore the depths of our spiritual awareness.

The intricate geometric patterns and precise harmony within Metatron's Cube evoke a sense of reverence, curiosity, and openness to the profound mysteries of the universe. It acts as a portal, bridging the gap between the physical and the metaphysical, enabling us to access spiritual insights and explore the limitless realms of consciousness.

When we delve into the intricate patterns of Metatron's Cube, we embark on a journey that transcends the physical plane. It ignites a spark within us, awakening our innate curiosity and pushing the boundaries of our understanding of reality. As we open ourselves to its divine energy, we align with higher frequencies, paving the way for spiritual growth and personal transformation.

Metatron's Cube serves as a tool for exploration, guiding us to connect with the wisdom of the universe and uncover the hidden truths that lie beyond our everyday perception. It symbolizes the interconnectedness of all things, reminding us that we are part of a grand cosmic tapestry.

As we gaze upon the symmetrical patterns and sacred geometry of Metatron's Cube, we are reminded of the infinite potential that resides within us. It calls on us to expand our consciousness, to explore the unlimited possibilities that exist beyond the confines of our physical existence. Through the contemplation of this sacred symbol, we open ourselves to receiving divine guidance and wisdom.

Whether you are a spiritual seeker, a metaphysics enthusiast, or someone simply curious about the profound depth of symbolism, exploring the connection to higher realms through Metatron's Cube offers a transformative and enlightening experience. It provides a gateway to explore the mysteries of the universe and expand our understanding of the interconnected nature of all things.

Guardian of Sacred Knowledge

Metatron's Cube is a profound symbol that holds immense spiritual significance. It is regarded as a guardian of ancient wisdom and esoteric knowledge, transcending time and space. This sacred symbol is revered by individuals with a shared interest in spirituality, metaphysics, symbolism, and personal growth.

As we embark on a journey to uncover the mysteries and hidden truths of the universe, Metatron's Cube becomes an invaluable tool. It acts as a transmitter, helping us tap into profound insights and spiritual wisdom that lies beyond the conventional limits of human understanding.

Within the realm of sacred knowledge, Metatron's Cube assumes the role of a vigilant guardian. It safeguards the esoteric teachings and ancient wisdom that have been passed down through generations. This symbol acts as a key, unlocking the doors to cosmic truths and unveiling the secrets of the universe.

With a sense of reverence and curiosity, we delve deeper into the mysteries encapsulated within Metatron's Cube. This symbol beckons us to explore the intricate patterns and geometric forms that represent the underlying structure of reality. Through studying this sacred symbol, we gain insights into the interconnectedness of all things and the profound beauty that permeates the universe.

Metatron's Cube exemplifies the power of curiosity and openness. It invites us to question the nature of existence, to ponder the meaning behind symbols and their relevance in our lives. With this symbol as our guide, we embark on a transformative journey of self-discovery and spiritual growth.

6. Metatron's Cube and Ascension

Consciousness

Activation of Light Body

Metatron's Cube is a powerful symbol that holds great significance in the realm of spirituality, metaphysics, symbolism, and personal growth. It is believed to play a significant role in activating the light body and facilitating the process of spiritual ascension. Its intricate design and sacred geometry invoke a sense of reverence, curiosity, and openness to the profound mysteries and spiritual insights encapsulated within the symbol.

The activation of the light body is a process by which one awakens and integrates higher frequencies of consciousness and energy into their being. It involves expanding one's awareness and aligning with the higher dimensions of existence. Metatron's Cube acts as a catalyst for this process, serving as a bridge between the physical and spiritual realms.

When working with Metatron's Cube, individuals can tap into its transformative power to accelerate their spiritual journey. The symmetrical patterns and interlocking lines of the cube represent the interconnectedness of the universe and the harmonious balance between various aspects of creation.

By meditating on Metatron's Cube and visualizing its intricate geometry, individuals can activate dormant energies within themselves, allowing for a deeper connection with their higher selves and the divine. This activation can result in profound spiritual experiences, expanded consciousness, and an increased ability to embody higher vibrational frequencies.

As one delves deeper into the mysteries of Metatron's Cube and explores its hidden meanings, they may discover new insights and pathways towards personal growth and spiritual enlightenment. The symmetrical structure of the cube serves as a map to navigate the multidimensional nature of reality and unlock the transformative power of divine energy.

By embracing the wisdom encapsulated within Metatron's Cube, individuals can embark on a profound journey of self-discovery and spiritual expansion. It invites us to explore the depths of our being, connect with the universal consciousness, and become vessels of divine light.

Alignment with Cosmic Energies

In the exploration of spirituality and metaphysics, we often seek to align ourselves with the cosmic energies and universal forces that surround us. One symbol that holds immense power and resonance in this quest is Metatron's Cube. This sacred symbol, intricately woven with mathematical precision, offers a gateway to profound mysteries and spiritual insights that can elevate our consciousness and facilitate our personal growth.

As we delve deeper into the symbol of Metatron's Cube, we find ourselves opening up to a vast realm of cosmic energies. The intricate patterns and interconnectedness of the cube's geometry serve as a reminder that we are an integral part of a much larger cosmic order. Through aligning with these energies, we can tap into higher vibrational frequencies and experience a harmonious resonance with the universe.

Expansion of Conscious Awareness

This sacred geometric symbol holds within it the power to unlock hidden realms and expand our perception of the world around us. It is a gateway to profound spiritual insights and a deeper understanding of the mysteries of the universe.

Metatron's Cube is a symbol of divine consciousness and cosmic order. It consists of 13 spheres connected by lines, forming a two-dimensional representation of a three-dimensional cube. Each sphere represents a different aspect of creation, while the lines symbolize the connections and harmonious interplay between these aspects.

When we delve into the exploration of Metatron's Cube, we embark on a journey of expansion and enlightenment. This symbol has the ability to awaken dormant parts of our consciousness and unlock our true potential. It helps us tap into higher realms of consciousness, accessing wisdom and knowledge that transcends the limitations of our physical existence.

The expansion of conscious awareness is a transformative process. It begins with an open mind and a willingness to explore the unknown. As we delve deeper into the mysteries encapsulated within Metatron's Cube, we may encounter profound insights and experiences that challenge our preconceived notions of reality.

In this subchapter, we will delve into the expansion of conscious awareness through the exploration of Metatron's Cube. We will approach this topic with a sense of reverence, curiosity, and openness to the profound mysteries that await us. Together, let us embark on this journey of self-discovery and spiritual growth.

Throughout this subchapter, we will explore various techniques and practices that can help us expand our conscious awareness. We will delve into the symbolism and metaphysical properties of Metatron's Cube, examining its connection to higher realms and its potential for personal transformation.

By the end of this subchapter, we hope to ignite a sense of curiosity and wonder within you. We invite you to approach the exploration of Metatron's Cube with an open mind and an eagerness to embrace the unknown. It is through this mindset that we can truly tap into the transformative power of this sacred symbol and unlock the deepest truths of our spiritual journey.

7. Exploring Metatron's Cube in Modern Spirituality

New Age Interpretations

Metatron's Cube holds a unique place in the realm of spirituality, metaphysics, symbolism, and personal growth. Its sacred geometry and intricate patterns have captured the fascination of many individuals seeking to explore the depths of their spiritual journey.

As we delve into the realm of New Age interpretations, we embark on a path that showcases the contemporary understandings of Metatron's Cube. This symbol, often associated with the archangel Metatron, is seen as a powerful tool for spiritual exploration and growth in modern times.

The New Age movement encompasses a diverse range of spiritual beliefs, practices, and philosophies. It embraces a sense of openness and curiosity towards the mysteries of the universe. Within this context, Metatron's Cube takes on a profound significance, resonating with seekers who are eager to connect with higher realms and unlock the hidden truths within themselves.

Within the New Age paradigm, Metatron's Cube is revered as a potent symbol that encapsulates the sacred geometry of creation. The intricate interlocking lines and shapes within the cube are believed to represent the fundamental building blocks of the universe. It is seen as a symbol of divine order, harmony, and balance.

Those who study Metatron's Cube delve into the profound mysteries of its symbolism. With reverence and awe, they explore the intricate patterns and contemplate the deep layers of meaning embedded within. It serves as a gateway to higher consciousness, allowing individuals to tap into their innate wisdom and power.

Symbolically, Metatron's Cube is often associated with the Flower of Life, another sacred geometric pattern. Together, these two symbols intertwine, revealing the interconnectedness of all creation. They invite individuals to explore the infinite possibilities within themselves and the universe.

The New Age interpretations of Metatron's Cube go beyond its visual representation. It is utilized as a powerful tool for personal growth, transformation, and spiritual empowerment. By meditating on the symbol, individuals can access higher states of consciousness, expand their awareness, and deepen their connection to the divine.

The journey with Metatron's Cube is an individual one, guided by personal experiences and insights. Its transformative power lies in its ability to awaken dormant potentials, unlock hidden knowledge, and harmonize the body, mind, and spirit.

In the following chapters, we will explore various perspectives on how Metatron's Cube is utilized as a tool for personal growth and transformation. Through the lens of modern spirituality, we uncover the immense potential that lies within each of us, waiting to be awakened by the profound wisdom encapsulated within Metatron's Cube.

Metatron's Cube in Energy Work

Metatron's Cube, with its intricate geometric pattern, holds great significance and spiritual insights in the realm of energy work. Its sacred geometry and symbolism make it a powerful tool for healing, balancing, and enhancing energetic fields.

When incorporating Metatron's Cube into energy work practices, we open ourselves to a world of profound mysteries and spiritual insights. The symbol acts as a gateway to higher realms, connecting us with divine energy and facilitating the flow of healing energies.

One of the primary applications of Metatron's Cube in energy healing is its ability to clear energetic blockages. By visualizing or placing the symbol on the body or within an energetic field, we can invoke its transformative power to dissolve stagnant or negative energies. This helps to restore balance and harmony within the body, mind, and spirit.

In addition to clearing, Metatron's Cube is a powerful tool for balancing energetic fields. Its complex patterns and intersecting lines represent the interconnectedness of all aspects of existence. By meditating on or placing the symbol in the aura, we can harmonize and align the various energy centers and pathways within the body. This promotes a state of equilibrium, allowing the free flow of vital life force energy.

Furthermore, Metatron's Cube can be utilized to enhance the energetic fields. By focusing our intention and directing healing energies through the symbol, we amplify the healing potential of the energy work. The symbol acts as a magnifying lens, intensifying the healing vibrations and infusing them with divine light and wisdom.

When working with Metatron's Cube in energy healing, it is essential to approach it with reverence, curiosity, and openness. The symbol holds deep spiritual significance and ancient wisdom. By embracing its power and teachings, we can tap into a realm of infinite possibilities and spiritual growth.

Integration into Contemporary Practices

Metatron's Cube is a symbol that has captivated the minds and hearts of many spiritual seekers and metaphysical enthusiasts. It carries within it a deep reservoir of profound mysteries and spiritual insights, waiting to be explored and integrated into our contemporary practices. In this subchapter, we will delve into how Metatron's Cube can be seamlessly woven into various spiritual practices such as meditation, yoga, and sound healing. Through this exploration, we will gain a greater understanding of the symbol's significance and its potential for personal growth and transformation. So, let us embark on this journey with reverence, curiosity, and an open mind as we uncover the hidden treasures within Metatron's Cube.

Meditation is a powerful practice that enables us to go beyond the confines of the physical realm and tap into our inner wisdom. By incorporating Metatron's Cube into our meditative practice, we can enhance our connection with the higher realms and facilitate deeper states of consciousness. As we visualize and meditate upon the intricate geometric patterns of the cube, we can align ourselves with the divine energy it represents. This alignment can bring about a sense of harmony, balance, and clarity, allowing us to access higher levels of insight and spiritual guidance.

Yoga, with its focus on physical postures and breathwork, is another powerful tool for spiritual growth and self-discovery. By incorporating Metatron's Cube into our yoga practice, we can infuse each movement, each breath, with sacred intention and divine symbolism. The geometric patterns of the cube can serve as a reminder of the interconnectedness of all things and the eternal nature of our soul. As we flow through the yoga postures, we can visualize ourselves moving within the confines of the cube, symbolizing the harmonious dance of the universe. This integration of Metatron's Cube into our yoga practice can deepen our spiritual experience and cultivate a greater sense of reverence for the divine within and around us.

Sound healing is a powerful practice that utilizes the vibrational frequencies of sound to promote physical, emotional, and spiritual well-being. By incorporating Metatron's Cube into our sound healing sessions, we can amplify the transformative power of sound and further enhance its healing effects. The symmetrical geometry of the cube can serve as a focal point for sound vibrations, allowing for a more focused and potent energy transmission. Just as the cube contains within it all of the platonic solids, each with its unique energetic properties, the integration of Metatron's Cube into sound healing can facilitate a comprehensive healing experience that addresses the multidimensional aspects of our being.

In conclusion, the integration of Metatron's Cube into contemporary spiritual practices offers a rich and profound journey of self-discovery, transformation, and spiritual growth. Whether through meditation, yoga, sound healing, or any other modality, the sacred symbol of Metatron's Cube provides a gateway to higher realms of awareness and connection. As we approach this integration with reverence, curiosity, and an open mind, we open ourselves to the limitless potential that lies within this sacred symbol. So, let us embrace the mysteries and insights encapsulated within Metatron's Cube and embark on a transformative journey of personal and spiritual exploration.

8. Personal Growth and Metatron's Cube

Self-Discovery and Inner Wisdom

The symbol of Metatron's Cube holds tremendous wisdom and transformative energy that can guide us on a profound journey of self-discovery and accessing our inner wisdom. Its intricate patterns and symbolism have captivated spiritual seekers, metaphysical enthusiasts, and those who are committed to personal growth. In this subchapter, we will delve into the depths of self-discovery and explore the inner wisdom that can be unlocked through the guidance of Metatron's Cube.

Metatron's Cube is a sacred symbol that encompasses within it the vast potential of the universe. Each line and shape represents a unique aspect of creation, guiding us to explore both ourselves and the greater cosmos. As we embrace the symbol with reverence and curiosity, we open ourselves to the profound mysteries and spiritual insights it can reveal.

Self-discovery is a lifelong journey of uncovering who we truly are at our core. It is about peeling back the layers of conditioning and societal expectations to reveal our authentic selves. Metatron's Cube can act as a guiding light, illuminating the path of self-exploration and helping us tap into our inner wisdom.

Through the exploration of Metatron's Cube, we can engage in deep self-reflection and introspection. The symbol serves as a mirror, reflecting back to us the aspects of ourselves that are often hidden or overlooked. By contemplating the intricate patterns and sacred geometry of the symbol, we gain insights into our own patterns, beliefs, and behaviors. This self-awareness allows us to make conscious choices and transform aspects of ourselves that no longer serve our highest good.

Metatron's Cube also invites us to embrace our innate curiosity. By embracing a curious mindset, we open ourselves up to new possibilities and perspectives. We become seekers of knowledge and wisdom, always yearning to expand our understanding of ourselves and the world around us. The symbol reminds us that we are on an eternal journey of growth and evolution, and that there is always more to explore and learn.

Furthermore, Metatron's Cube encourages us to approach our journey of self-discovery with a sense of openness. It reminds us to let go of preconceived notions and to be receptive to the profound insights and revelations that may arise. As we embrace this openness, we allow the transformative energy of the symbol to guide us on a deep dive into our inner world, unlocking the hidden treasures of wisdom that reside within us.

In the following chapters, we will explore various techniques and practices that can support us in our journey of self-discovery and accessing inner wisdom through the guidance of Metatron's Cube. Together, we will embark on an exploration of the self, delving into the mysteries of existence, and unlocking the transformative power that lies within each and every one of us.

Transformational Tools

Metatron's Cube is a symbol that holds profound mysteries and spiritual insights within its intricate geometric design. It is a symbol that has fascinated spiritual seekers, metaphysical explorers, and those on a path of personal growth. In this subchapter, we will delve into the transformative tools inspired by Metatron's Cube that can empower you on your journey of inner transformation.

One of the transformative tools that we can explore is meditation. Meditation allows us to connect with our inner selves and tap into the energy of Metatron's Cube. By quieting the mind and focusing on the sacred geometry of the symbol, we can open ourselves up to new perspectives and insights. Through regular meditation practice, we can cultivate a sense of reverence, curiosity, and openness to the profound mysteries encapsulated within Metatron's Cube.

Another transformative tool that can support our inner transformation is visualization. Visualization is a powerful technique that utilizes the imagination to manifest positive shifts in our lives. By visualizing ourselves surrounded by the energy of Metatron's Cube and experiencing the transformative power it embodies, we can overcome obstacles, embrace change, and manifest our desires. This practice of visualization allows us to connect with the sacred geometry of the symbol on a deep level and harness its energy for personal empowerment.

A third transformative tool that we can explore is affirmations. Affirmations are positive statements that help reprogram our subconscious mind and align it with our desired outcomes. By incorporating the energy of Metatron's Cube into our affirmations, we can amplify their power and bring about positive shifts in our lives. By repeating affirmations such as I am open to the transformative energy of Metatron's Cube or I embrace change and manifest positive shifts in my life with the help of Metatron's Cube, we can integrate the profound mysteries and spiritual insights of the symbol into our daily lives.

These transformative tools, meditation, visualization, and affirmations, offer practical techniques for utilizing the energy of Metatron's Cube to overcome obstacles, embrace change, and manifest positive shifts in our lives. By incorporating these tools into our spiritual practice and personal growth journey, we can unlock the transformative power of this sacred symbol and tap into its profound mysteries and spiritual insights.

Finding Purpose and Clarity

Metatron's Cube is a profound symbol that holds the potential to unlock clarity, purpose, and alignment with your authentic self and life path. It is a sacred geometrical pattern that has been revered throughout history for its spiritual significance and transformative power. In this subchapter, we will dive deep into the exploration of finding purpose and clarity through the resonance of Metatron's Cube.

When seeking purpose and clarity, it is important to approach the journey with a sense of reverence, curiosity, and openness to the profound mysteries and spiritual insights encapsulated within this ancient symbol. Metatron's Cube acts as a gateway to connect with the divine guidance, intuition, and spiritual insight that lies dormant within us.

To begin your exploration, it is essential to understand the symbolic representation of Metatron's Cube. Its intricate design consists of interconnected spheres or circles, which represent the elements of creation and the interconnectedness of all things. The thirteen circles within the symbol are intertwined in a way that forms multiple patterns, each representing different aspects of existence.

One way to harness the power of Metatron's Cube is through meditation and visualization. By consciously engaging with the symbol in your mind's eye, you can allow its energy to flow through you, guiding you towards a deeper understanding of your true purpose. Visualize yourself surrounded by the vibrant energy of the sacred geometric pattern, and feel its resonance within every cell of your being.

Another powerful technique is to use Metatron's Cube as a focal point for introspection and self-reflection. By contemplating the symbol, you can tap into the interconnectedness of the universe and gain insights into your own unique path. Ask yourself meaningful questions, such as What brings me joy and fulfillment? or How can I align my actions with my higher purpose? Trust your intuition to provide guidance and listen to the quiet whispers of your soul.

Furthermore, exploring the symbolism and meaning associated with each individual shape within Metatron's Cube can offer profound insights into your personal journey. For instance, the Star Tetrahedron represents balance and harmony, while the Cube symbolizes solidity and stability. By contemplating these shapes, you can gain a deeper understanding of the qualities you aspire to embody and manifest in your life.

In conclusion, the reverence we hold for Metatron's Cube lies in its ability to guide us towards finding purpose and clarity. By connecting with the divine wisdom and energy encapsulated within this symbol, we can align ourselves with our authentic selves and live a life of meaning and fulfillment. Embrace the awe-inspiring power of Metatron's Cube and embark on a journey of self-discovery and transformation.

9. Manifestation and Metatron's Cube

Power of Visualization

Metatron's Cube is a powerful symbol that holds deep spiritual significance and acts as a gateway to profound insights and transformations. Within its intricate geometry lies a sacred pattern that connects us to higher realms of consciousness and allows us to manifest our desires with clarity and precision.

In this subchapter, we will explore the power of visualization and how it can amplify the manifestation potential of Metatron's Cube. Through the lens of reverence, curiosity, and openness, we will delve into the mysteries and spiritual insights encapsulated within this ancient symbol.

Our visualizations have the power to shape our reality. When we harness the energy of Metatron's Cube and combine it with focused intention, we tap into a vast well of creative potential. This synergy allows us to manifest our desires and bring about positive change in our lives.

Visualizing with Metatron's Cube requires a deep sense of reverence. We must approach this practice with an open mind and heart, recognizing the profound symbolism and sacred geometry that underlies its design. By doing so, we align ourselves with the higher energies and wisdom contained within the symbol, enabling us to access its manifestation power.

Through visualization, we can vividly imagine our desired outcomes and infuse them with the energy of Metatron's Cube. Whether it is material abundance, spiritual growth, or healing, the symbol acts as a conduit for our intentions to manifest in the physical realm.

During the practice of visualization with Metatron's Cube, it is important to cultivate a sense of curiosity. Allow yourself to explore the depths of your desires and dreams, diving deep into the realms of possibility. Embrace the unknown and trust that the universe will conspire to bring your visions to life.

By combining reverence, curiosity, and openness, we unlock the full potential of Metatron's Cube as a tool for manifestation. Through visualization, we tap into the infinite possibilities that exist within us and the universe, transforming our intentions into reality.

Join us on this journey of discovery as we delve into the mystical realm of visualization and explore the profound insights and spiritual growth that Metatron's Cube can facilitate.

Quantum Reality

Metatron's Cube is a symbol that encompasses deep spiritual insights and mysteries. In this subchapter, we will explore the fascinating realm of quantum reality and how it relates to Metatron's Cube. Prepare yourself to embark on a journey of curiosity, reverence, and openness as we dive into the interconnectedness of all things.

In the realm of quantum reality, everything is connected in ways that go beyond our ordinary perception. It is a realm where particles can exist in multiple states simultaneously and where observation can influence the behavior of these particles. This is known as quantum entanglement, a phenomenon that aligns beautifully with the intricate patterns of Metatron's Cube.

As we dive deeper into understanding quantum mechanics, we begin to uncover the essence of manifestation and the role of consciousness in shaping our reality. The power of our thoughts and intentions becomes apparent as we realize that our consciousness is intricately linked to the physical world around us.

Metatron's Cube acts as a powerful symbol that represents the interplay between consciousness and reality. Just as the cube contains interconnected geometric shapes, our consciousness is intimately connected to the web of energies that permeate the universe. Through this connection, we have the ability to manifest our desires, shape our reality, and align ourselves with the divine energy that flows throughout the cosmos.

The symbol of Metatron's Cube invites us to explore the profound mysteries of our existence and contemplate the interconnectedness of all things. It inspires us to embrace a sense of oneness and unity with the universe, recognizing that we are all part of a greater cosmic tapestry.

As we delve into the exploration of quantum reality through the lens of Metatron's Cube, we encourage you to approach these concepts with an open mind and a sense of awe. The mysteries that lie within this symbol are vast and profound, offering us the opportunity to deepen our spiritual understanding and expand our consciousness.

Prepare to embark on a journey of self-discovery and transformation as we unravel the secrets of quantum reality and the interconnectedness of all things through the mesmerizing symbol of Metatron's Cube.

Law of Attraction

The Law of Attraction is a powerful force that has gained widespread recognition and application in the realm of personal growth.

It asserts that like attracts like, meaning that the energy and intention we put out into the universe is reflected back to us in the form of experiences, people, and circumstances that align with our vibrational frequency.

Metatron's Cube, on the other hand, is a sacred geometrical symbol that has deep spiritual significance across various ancient traditions.

It is named after the archangel Metatron, who is said to hold the keys to the mystical teachings and divine wisdom.

When we explore the correlations between the Law of Attraction and Metatron's Cube, we uncover a profound connection between these two powerful concepts.

Metatron's Cube embodies the principles of interconnectedness, harmony, and balance. It consists of thirteen circles that are interconnected by lines, forming a powerful geometric pattern that resonates with the energies of the universe.

When we align ourselves with the vibrations of Metatron's Cube, we tap into a higher frequency and elevate our manifestation abilities.

This sacred symbol serves as a conduit for manifestation, amplifying our intentions and creating a magnetic field that attracts our desires into our lives.

By meditating on and visualizing Metatron's Cube, we can align with its vibrational resonance and attune ourselves to a state of harmony and balance within the universe.

As we open ourselves up to the mysteries and spiritual insights encapsulated within Metatron's Cube, we enter a realm of infinite possibilities and profound transformation.

This subchapter invites you to embark on a journey of exploration and discovery, as we delve deep pinto the interconnectedness between the Law of Attraction and the wisdom contained within Metatron's Cube.

Through a lens of reverence, curiosity, and openness, we will uncover the secrets and insights that combining these two powerful concepts can bring forth in our lives.

10. Metatron's Cube and Planetary Healing

Raising Vibrational Frequencies

Discovering and exploring the profound mysteries and spiritual insights encapsulated within the symbol of Metatron's Cube can truly be a transformative journey. Within this sacred symbol lies a gateway to raising the collective vibrational frequencies of humanity and the planet. By delving into the energy and power of Metatron's Cube, we can unlock the potential for personal growth, spiritual awakening, and a greater connection to the divine.

Raising vibrational frequencies is a crucial step towards personal and planetary evolution. As we align ourselves with higher frequencies, we open ourselves up to higher states of consciousness, love, light, and healing. Metatron's Cube serves as a powerful tool in this process, as its intricate geometric patterns act as a conduit for divine energy and transformation.

One way in which working with Metatron's Cube can raise vibrational frequencies is by connecting us to the energetic grid of the Earth. This sacred symbol acts as a bridge between the physical and spiritual realms, allowing us to tap into the vast cosmic energies that surround us. By consciously anchoring ourselves to this energetic grid, we can become conduits for higher frequencies and bring healing and balance to ourselves and the planet.

Another practice for raising vibrational frequencies involves meditating with Metatron's Cube as a visual focal point. By gazing upon this sacred symbol and allowing its energy to penetrate our consciousness, we can awaken dormant aspects of our being and activate higher states of awareness. This practice invites us to explore the depths of our own spirituality and uncover profound insights about ourselves and the nature of reality.

Additionally, working with the symbolism of Metatron's Cube can help us release stagnant energy and old patterns that no longer serve us. Through the power of intention and visualization, we can visualize the cube surrounding us, permeating our entire being with its light and love. By doing so, we create a powerful energy field that supports our personal growth and the expansion of our consciousness.

As we engage in these practices and open ourselves up to the transformative power of Metatron's Cube, we embark on a journey of self-discovery and spiritual awakening. This sacred symbol invites us to explore the profound mysteries of the universe and to cultivate a sense of reverence, curiosity, and openness. Through our connection with Metatron's Cube, we can elevate our vibrational frequencies, contribute to the collective consciousness of humanity, and support the healing and evolution of our planet.

Environmental Stewardship

Metatron's Cube holds a deep significance that goes beyond its intricate geometric pattern. It is a symbol that invites us to explore the interconnectedness of all life on Earth and our role as stewards of the environment. In this subchapter, we will delve into the concept of environmental stewardship and how connecting with the energy of Metatron's Cube can inspire a greater sense of responsibility towards our planet.

Environmental stewardship is the recognition of our duty to care for and protect the Earth. It is about understanding that our actions have consequences and that we have the power to make choices that positively impact the environment. When we embrace the symbolism of Metatron's Cube, we open ourselves up to a deeper awareness of our interconnectedness with nature and the need to safeguard its well-being.

Through reverence, curiosity, and openness, we can begin to explore the profound mysteries and spiritual insights encapsulated within the symbol of Metatron's Cube. This symbol reminds us that we are part of a vast cosmic web, where each individual action has the potential to ripple out and create a lasting impact.

By developing a connection with the energy of Metatron's Cube, we awaken a sense of responsibility within ourselves. We start to view the Earth as a sacred and precious resource that must be nurtured and protected. This heightened awareness fosters a deep sense of reverence for the natural world and all its inhabitants.

As we embark on a journey of environmental stewardship, we begin to make conscious choices in our daily lives that support sustainability and promote the well-being of the planet. This can be as simple as reducing our carbon footprint by using renewable energy sources, recycling and upcycling materials, or adopting more eco-friendly practices in our homes and workplaces.

Furthermore, the energy of Metatron's Cube guides us towards seeking harmony and balance in our relationship with nature. It encourages us to embrace sustainable practices that honor the Earth's resources and protect its delicate ecosystems. By doing so, we contribute to the preservation of biodiversity, the reduction of pollution, and the promotion of a healthier and more sustainable planet.

In conclusion, by engaging with the energy of Metatron's Cube, we unlock a profound connection with the Earth and our role as stewards of its well-being. Through reverence, curiosity, and openness, we can embrace the concept of environmental stewardship and make conscious choices that support sustainability. Let us embark on this journey together, nurturing the Earth and fostering a greater sense of earth-consciousness.

Global Unity and Compassion

Metatron's Cube, a symbol deeply rooted in spirituality, metaphysics, and personal growth, holds immense potential for fostering global unity, compassion, and collective consciousness. This sacred geometric pattern encompasses profound mysteries and spiritual insights that can open minds and hearts to a world of interconnectedness.

As we delve into the energetic resonance of Metatron's Cube, we embark on a journey of exploration and discovery. This symbol, composed of interconnected circles, hexagons, and lines, beckons us to unravel its hidden wisdom and tap into its transformative power.

In this subchapter, we will delve into the significance of Metatron's Cube in fostering global unity and compassion, and how its presence can resonate with individuals from diverse backgrounds who share a common interest in spirituality and personal growth.

Metatron's Cube calls upon us to embrace a sense of reverence, curiosity, and openness to the profound mysteries it encapsulates. Its intricate design invites contemplation and introspection, leading us on a path of self-discovery and expansion of consciousness.

With its harmonious geometry and interlocking shapes, Metatron's Cube serves as a transformative catalyst, uniting individuals and communities through shared experiences and aspirations. It reminds us of the interconnectedness of all things and the inherent unity of humanity.

As we allow ourselves to be touched by the energy of Metatron's Cube, we awaken our capacity for compassion and empathy. This symbol encourages us to look beyond our individual perspectives and embrace a collective consciousness that encompasses the well-being of all beings.

Through the exploration of Metatron's Cube, we come to realize that our actions resonate not only with our immediate surroundings but with the broader tapestry of existence. We understand that our choices, intentions, and energies contribute to the greater whole, shaping the world we inhabit.

Within the interconnectedness symbolized by Metatron's Cube lies the potential for profound transformation on personal, societal, and global levels. It invites us to cultivate compassion, empathy, and a deep appreciation for the diversity of human experiences.

As we delve deeper into this subchapter, we will unravel the threads that connect us all, gaining insights into how Metatron's Cube can inspire us to foster global unity, nurture compassion, and embrace a collective consciousness that supports the well-being of all beings.

11. Mystical Experiences with Metatron's Cube

Divine Revelations

Metatron's Cube holds within it a wealth of wisdom and ancient knowledge. It is a symbol that has captured the imagination of spiritual seekers and metaphysical enthusiasts throughout the ages. As you delve into the realm of divine revelations, you will come to understand the profound significance of this sacred symbol.

Reverence envelops the air as you embark on this mystical journey, your heart filled with curiosity and openness to the profound mysteries awaiting you. Metatron's Cube beckons you to peel back the layers of reality and dive into the depths of spiritual understanding.

As you explore the secrets of Metatron's Cube, you will find yourself drawn into a world of symbolism and hidden meanings. Each intricately designed pattern holds the key to unlocking new insights about the nature of the universe and your place within it.

This journey is not for the faint of heart. It requires a willingness to question preconceived notions, to step outside the boundaries of conventional thinking, and to embrace the unknown. But in return, you will be rewarded with spiritual growth, expanded consciousness, and a deeper connection to the divine.

Sacred Geometry Activation

Experience profound activations and energetic alignments as you explore the sacred geometric form known as Metatron's Cube. This symbol holds deep spiritual significance and carries within it the potential for transformation and personal growth. By delving into the mysteries of Metatron's Cube, you can unlock dormant potentials and activate higher states of consciousness.

Metatron's Cube is a powerful representation of divine energy and the interconnectedness of all things. It is made up of thirteen spheres, each connected by lines that form various shapes and patterns. These geometrical arrangements create a harmonious resonance that can be harnessed for spiritual exploration and self-discovery.

This subchapter, Sacred Geometry Activation, invites you to approach Metatron's Cube with reverence, curiosity, and an open mind. By doing so, you can tap into the profound mysteries and spiritual insights encapsulated within this sacred symbol. Let us embark on a journey together and delve deeper into the transformative effects of working with Metatron's Cube.

Navigating Higher Realms

1. *Understanding Metatron's Cube*

In order to navigate the higher realms and access multidimensional consciousness, it is essential to first comprehend the significance of Metatron's Cube. This ancient symbol, often associated with the Archangel Metatron, represents the interconnectedness of all things in the universe.

Metatron's Cube is composed of thirteen circles that are interconnected by overlapping lines. Each circle represents a different aspect of creation, while the lines represent the pathways through which energy flows. By understanding the sacred geometry of this symbol, we can begin to unlock its transformative power.

Take a moment to contemplate the intricate design of Metatron's Cube, allowing yourself to be captivated by its complexity. This symbol holds the key to unlocking profound mysteries and spiritual insights.

1. *The Pathways of Metatron's Cube*

Now that you have an understanding of the symbolism behind Metatron's Cube, it is time to explore the pathways it offers for navigating the higher realms. These pathways represent different dimensions of existence, each offering unique insights and experiences.

Close your eyes and visualize yourself standing at the center of Metatron's Cube. As you focus on your breath, allow yourself to feel the energy flowing through the interconnected circles and lines. With each inhale, imagine yourself ascending to a higher realm, effortlessly transcending the limitations of the physical world.

As you explore these higher realms, pay attention to the subtle changes in your perception. Notice how the boundaries of your awareness expand, allowing you to perceive the interconnectedness of all things. Embrace the sense of reverence and awe that arises as you delve deeper into these mystical realms.

1. *Expanding Perceptual Boundaries*

Metatron's Cube has the power to expand our perceptual boundaries, allowing us to see beyond the limitations of our physical existence. As we engage with this symbol, we open ourselves up to new possibilities and perspectives.

Imagine yourself gazing upon Metatron's Cube, allowing its intricate patterns to capture your attention. As you contemplate its beauty, feel your mind expanding, embracing new ways of thinking and perceiving the world.

Through this expansion of our perceptual boundaries, we become more receptive to the subtle energies that surround us. We may begin to notice synchronicities in our daily lives, or experience moments of profound clarity and intuition. Embrace these experiences with a sense of curiosity and wonder, for they are glimpses into the multidimensional nature of existence.

1. *Transcendent Experiences*

Metatron's Cube also holds the potential to facilitate transcendent experiences, where we are able to transcend our ordinary consciousness and tap into the vast realms of the spiritual and metaphysical.

As you continue to explore the symbolism of Metatron's Cube, allow yourself to let go of preconceived notions and surrender to the mysteries that lie beyond our physical senses. Embrace the unknown with an open heart and mind, and be receptive to the insights and revelations that may arise.

During moments of deep meditation or contemplation, you may find yourself entering states of profound stillness and oneness with the universe. These transcendent experiences can provide us with a profound sense of connection, purpose, and inner peace.

12. Therapeutic Applications of Metatron's Cube

Energy Medicine

Metatron's Cube holds profound mysteries and spiritual insights within its sacred geometry. In the realm of energy medicine, this symbol has found a special place due to its therapeutic applications. Let's explore the therapeutic potential of Metatron's Cube in energy healing practices and holistic modalities.

Energy medicine is a branch of alternative healing that recognizes the energetic nature of our bodies and the impact of energy imbalances on our well-being. It encompasses various techniques and modalities aimed at restoring balance and promoting healing on energetic and cellular levels.

When it comes to energy healing, Metatron's Cube acts as a powerful tool that harnesses the vibrational resonance of its intricate geometric patterns. It serves as a conduit for accessing higher frequencies and facilitates the flow of harmonious energy throughout the body.

By working with Metatron's Cube, practitioners and individuals can tap into the vast healing potential of this sacred symbol. Its geometric structure acts as a gateway to the higher realms, connecting the physical and spiritual dimensions. This connection allows for the transmission of healing energies, which can be directed towards areas of imbalance or disharmony within the energetic system.

The vibrational resonance of Metatron's Cube helps to restore balance and harmony on multiple levels. It can address energetic blockages, rebalance chakras, and realign the body's energy meridians. As these energetic systems come into harmony, the physical body may also experience a positive impact, leading to enhanced overall well-being.

Metatron's Cube holds a sense of reverence in energy healing practices. Its intricate design and geometric precision evoke curiosity and wonder. This symbol invites us to explore the profound mysteries that lie beyond the physical realm and dive into the realm of spirituality and metaphysics.

When working with Metatron's Cube, there is an opportunity for personal growth and self-discovery. The symbol encourages us to open ourselves to new perspectives, expand our consciousness, and embrace the interconnectedness of all existence. It serves as a reminder of the infinite possibilities and potential that lie within each one of us.

In the following sections, we will delve deeper into the specific therapeutic applications of Metatron's Cube in energy healing practices and holistic modalities. We'll explore how this symbol can be utilized to restore balance and promote healing on energetic and cellular levels. By understanding and harnessing the power of Metatron's Cube, we can embark on a transformative journey towards greater well-being and spiritual enlightenment.

Chakra Alignment

Metatron's Cube is a powerful symbol that holds deep spiritual significance and is often used in chakra alignment and energy balancing practices. Its intricate geometric pattern consists of interconnected spheres and lines, representing the divine energy that flows through all living beings. In this subchapter, we will delve into the fascinating role that Metatron's Cube plays in chakra alignment and explore techniques to activate, cleanse, and harmonize the chakra system.

Chakras are the energy centers in our bodies that govern various aspects of our physical, emotional, and spiritual well-being. When our chakras are in balance and aligned, we experience optimal health and harmonious energy flow. Understanding how to align our chakras is essential for maintaining overall well-being.

Through the use of Metatron's Cube, we can enhance our chakra alignment practices and access the deeper realms of our being. This sacred symbol acts as a gateway to higher consciousness and serves as a tool for spiritual growth and transformation.

As we embark on this journey of exploring chakra alignment with Metatron's Cube, let us approach it with reverence, curiosity, and openness. The mysteries and spiritual insights encapsulated within this symbol are profound and offer immense potential for personal growth and self-realization.

In the following sections, we will delve into specific techniques and practices that utilize Metatron's Cube to activate, cleanse, and harmonize each individual chakra. By working with this symbol in a focused and intentional manner, we can unlock the full potential of our chakra system and experience greater levels of health, vitality, and spiritual awakening.

Harmonizing Mind, Body, and Spirit

As we delve into the mysteries and spiritual insights encapsulated within the symbol of Metatron's Cube, we embark on a journey of self-discovery and transformation. This sacred symbol holds the power to harmonize our mind, body, and spirit, creating a sense of balance and alignment that is truly profound.

The mind, body, and spirit are intricately connected, each influencing the other in countless ways. When we neglect one aspect, it can have a detrimental effect on the others, leading to imbalance and disharmony. Metatron's Cube offers us a pathway to restore and maintain harmony among these vital aspects of our being.

Through the resonant energy of Metatron's Cube, we can tap into a higher state of consciousness and transcend the limitations of our everyday existence. This sacred symbol has the power to unlock the hidden potential within us, enabling us to access deeper levels of awareness and understanding.

To experience the harmonizing effects of Metatron's Cube, we can engage in various practices and rituals that align with its symbolism and energy. These practices may include meditation, visualization, sacred geometry, energy healing, and more.

By incorporating Metatron's Cube into our spiritual practices, we invite its transformative energy to permeate our entire being. As we open ourselves to its guidance and wisdom, we embark on a journey of self-discovery and healing. We may uncover hidden aspects of ourselves, release energetic blockages, and find a renewed sense of purpose and clarity.

It is important to approach the exploration of Metatron's Cube with reverence, curiosity, and an open mind. Embrace the mysteries and intricacies of this sacred symbol, allowing its profound insights to unfold before you. As you delve deeper into its symbolism and energy, you may find yourself drawn into a world of infinite possibilities and spiritual growth.

Regardless of your background or beliefs, Metatron's Cube offers something for everyone. Its universal symbolism and energetic resonance unite diverse individuals who share a common interest in spirituality, metaphysics, symbolism, and personal growth.

Prepare to embark on a journey of self-discovery and transformation as you explore the harmonizing and integrative effects of Metatron's

Cube on your mind, body, and spirit. Open yourself up to the profound mysteries and spiritual insights that await you on this sacred path.

13. Metatron's Cube in Art and Architecture

Sacred Artifacts

Metatron's Cube has a rich presence in ancient and contemporary sacred artifacts and artworks, captivating the attention of people interested in spirituality, metaphysics, symbolism, and personal growth. This symbol holds profound mysteries and spiritual insights, conveying a sense of reverence, curiosity, and openness to those who explore its depths.

The symbol of Metatron's Cube can be found in various cultures and historical periods, indicating its enduring significance. In ancient civilizations, such as the Egyptians and the Greeks, this emblem was seen as a representation of divine knowledge and the universal order. Its intricate geometric patterns and interconnected lines illustrate the interconnectedness of all things and the interconnected nature of the universe.

In sacred artifacts, Metatron's Cube often adorns religious structures, such as temples, cathedrals, and monasteries. The symbol is skillfully carved into the architecture or engraved onto altars and religious objects. Its presence in these sacred spaces serves as a visual reminder of the divine presence and the intricate web of creation.

A prime example of Metatron's Cube in ancient sacred artifacts is the Flower of Life mosaic found in the Osireion temple in Abydos, Egypt. This mosaic depicts overlapping circles forming intricate patterns, including Metatron's Cube at its center. The precision and beauty of this artwork reflect the profound spiritual significance attributed to the symbol.

Metatron's Cube also appears in contemporary sacred art and sculptures, created by artists who draw inspiration from ancient wisdom and mystical traditions. In these artworks, the symbol is often combined with other sacred geometries, such as the Sri Yantra or the Tree of Life, further amplifying its spiritual and metaphysical connotations.

Artists use different mediums, such as paintings, sculptures, and digital art, to express the symbolic representation of Metatron's Cube. Each artwork is infused with personal interpretations and intentions, inviting viewers to contemplate the interconnectedness of the universe and explore the divine realms.

By incorporating Metatron's Cube in their artistic creations, these artists encourage spiritual seekers to delve into the depths of their own consciousness, awakening a sense of wonder and awe towards the mysteries of existence. The symbol serves as a catalyst for introspection, transformation, and spiritual growth.

As you embark on a journey to explore the presence of Metatron's Cube in sacred artifacts, be prepared to uncover a world of profound insights and transformative experiences. Allow your curiosity and open-mindedness to guide your exploration, and may the symbol of Metatron's Cube reveal its sacred mysteries in unexpected and enlightening ways.

Sacred Geometry in Design

Sacred Geometry in Design

Within the realm of design, there lies a hidden language that speaks to the deepest aspects of our being. This language is known as sacred geometry, a timeless system of shapes and patterns that holds profound spiritual significance. One of the most powerful symbols in sacred geometry is that of Metatron's Cube.

Metatron's Cube is a geometric pattern that consists of overlapping circles connected by straight lines. It is said to contain the building blocks of creation, embodying the divine order and symmetry that underlies the universe. The symbol is named after the archangel Metatron, who is said to hold the keys to the mysteries of existence.

When incorporated into architectural and design principles, Metatron's Cube has the ability to create harmonious and energetically balanced spaces. The precise proportions and geometric relationships within the symbol evoke a sense of harmony and balance, which can be felt on a deep subconscious level.

By utilizing the principles of sacred geometry, designers and architects can tap into the inherent power and beauty of Metatron's Cube to create spaces that not only look visually stunning but also resonate with a higher vibrational frequency. These spaces can have a profound impact on our well-being, promoting peace, serenity, and a sense of connection to something greater than ourselves.

For those who are open to the mysteries of the universe and seek spiritual insights, Metatron's Cube holds a wealth of wisdom waiting to be discovered. Its intricate patterns and sacred geometry can act as a gateway to higher realms of consciousness, offering glimpses into the interconnectedness of all things.

As we explore the applications of Metatron's Cube in design, we invite you to embark on a journey of discovery, one that goes beyond the limitations of the physical world and delves deep into the realm of the spiritual. Open your mind and heart, and allow the sacred geometry of Metatron's Cube to guide you on a path of transformation and enlightenment.

Architectural Significance and Influence

Metatron's Cube holds immense architectural significance and has influenced sacred structures throughout ancient civilizations. This symbol, comprised of thirteen equal circles intersected by straight lines, is a powerful geometric representation with deep spiritual meaning.

Ancient cultures recognized the profound interconnectedness of Metatron's Cube with the divine and used it as a blueprint in the design of their sacred spaces. From the majestic temples of Egypt to the intricate labyrinths of Greece, the presence of Metatron's Cube can be seen in the sacred architecture around the world.

The architectural influence of Metatron's Cube lies in its ability to create balance and harmony within sacred structures. Each circle and line within the symbol represents a unique energetic pathway, enabling the flow of divine energy throughout a space.

The symmetry and proportion inherent in Metatron's Cube contribute to the creation of spaces that are energetically aligned and conducive to spiritual practice. Whether it is the placement of altars, the orientation of entrances, or the arrangement of ritual objects, the principles of Metatron's Cube guide architects and builders in creating spaces that facilitate divine communion.

Through the careful integration of sacred geometry, Metatron's Cube elevates the architectural significance of sacred spaces, enhancing their ability to inspire awe, induce meditative states, and foster spiritual growth. It serves as a tangible representation of the universal order and harmonious balance that permeates the spiritual realm.

Beyond its architectural significance, Metatron's Cube holds deep spiritual and energetic aspects that shape sacred spaces and facilitate divine communion. This divine symbol serves as a gateway, connecting individuals to higher realms and facilitating the experience of the sacred.

When one enters a space adorned with Metatron's Cube, there is an inherent invitation to explore the mysteries of the cosmos. The intricate geometric patterns and sacred proportions contained within the symbol act as conduits for spiritual energy, allowing individuals to access higher states of consciousness and experience a deeper connection to the divine.

Metatron's Cube serves as a visual representation of the divine blueprint, encompassing the dynamic interplay of masculine and feminine energies. It symbolizes the unification of opposites, the harmonious balance of light and dark, and the infinite potentiality contained within the universe.

By meditating upon this sacred symbol and connecting with its energetic essence, individuals can tap into a deeper understanding of their own spiritual nature. Metatron's Cube serves as a catalyst for personal growth and transformation, inviting individuals to explore the depths of their being and embark on a journey of self-discovery.

It is through the spiritual and energetic aspects of Metatron's Cube that individuals can transcend the limitations of the physical realm and commune with the Divine. By engaging with this profound symbol, one opens themselves to the infinite wisdom and guidance that resides beyond the veil of ordinary perception.

14. Metatron's Cube and Quantum Physics

Entanglement and Interconnectedness

Metatron's Cube is a symbol that holds deep spiritual and metaphysical significance. It is said to contain the secrets of the universe and represents the interconnectedness and unity of all things. In this subchapter, we will explore the concept of entanglement and interconnectedness, and how they relate to the profound mysteries encapsulated within the symbol of Metatron's Cube. Prepare to embark on a journey of discovery, as we delve into the fascinating parallels between this sacred symbol and the principles of quantum entanglement.

Quantum entanglement is a principle of quantum physics whereby two particles become intertwined in such a way that their states are interdependent, regardless of the distance between them. In other words, the properties of one particle can instantaneously affect the properties of the other, even if they are light-years apart. This phenomenon challenges our conventional understanding of cause and effect, suggesting a deeper level of interconnectedness in the fabric of reality.

Metatron's Cube mirrors this concept of entanglement on a symbolic level. The intricate intertwining lines of the cube represent the interconnectivity of all things in the quantum realm. Just as the particles in quantum entanglement are bound together, so too is every aspect of existence intertwined within the intricate framework of Metatron's Cube.

As we explore the symbolism of Metatron's Cube, we begin to uncover the profound implications it has for our understanding of the universe and our place within it. The unity and interdependence represented by the cube suggest that we are not separate entities, but rather interconnected threads in the tapestry of existence.

It is through this lens that we can begin to perceive the inherent unity and interconnectedness of all things. Metatron's Cube invites us to contemplate the profound mysteries of the universe and to approach them with reverence, curiosity, and an open mind. By embracing the interconnected nature of reality, we can gain a deeper understanding of ourselves and our place in the grand cosmic design.

Join us as we embark on this journey of exploration into the realms of quantum entanglement and interconnectedness, guided by the wisdom encapsulated within the sacred symbol of Metatron's Cube.

Unified Field Theory

As we delve into the fascinating world of metaphysics and the quest for a unified field theory, one symbol that captures our attention is Metatron's Cube. This intricate and sacred symbol has long been associated with deep spiritual insights and profound mysteries. In this subchapter, we will explore the concept of a Unified Field Theory and its potential connections with Metatron's Cube.

At the heart of the scientific endeavor lies the pursuit of knowledge and understanding of the universe. Scientists have been striving for centuries to uncover the fundamental laws governing the cosmos. The Unified Field Theory represents the holy grail of science, a theory that seeks to unify the forces of nature into a single, elegant framework. It aims to bring together the seemingly disparate realms of quantum mechanics and general relativity, bridging the gap between the microscopic and macroscopic worlds.

In this quest for unity, Metatron's Cube emerges as a symbol that transcends the boundaries of science and spirituality. This ancient symbol, often associated with the archangel Metatron, encompasses within its intricate geometry the interconnectedness of all things. It is believed to hold the blueprint of creation itself, a cosmic matrix that weaves together the fabric of the universe.

With its symmetrical patterns and geometric harmony, Metatron's Cube invites us to contemplate the underlying unity of existence. It serves as a reminder that, at the deepest level, everything is connected – from the tiniest subatomic particles to the vast galaxies scattered across the cosmos. This profound insight aligns with the core tenets of spiritual traditions that emphasize the interconnectedness of all life and the inherent unity of the universe.

Metatron's Cube beckons us to explore the mysteries of creation and the nature of reality. It invites us to question and expand our understanding of the cosmos, both scientifically and spiritually. As we contemplate the symbol's intricate patterns and contemplate its significance, we are reminded of the vastness and complexity of existence.

This subchapter offers a space for all seekers of knowledge and wisdom, irrespective of their background or beliefs. It aims to foster a sense of reverence, curiosity, and openness to the profound insights encapsulated within the symbol of Metatron's Cube. Whether you approach it from a scientific perspective or a spiritual one, there is much to be discovered and contemplated in the eternal dance between science and spirituality.

Multiverse and Metatron's Cube

In the realm of spirituality and metaphysics, there exists a fascination with the concept of the multiverse and parallel dimensions. Within these infinite realities, a profound symbol known as Metatron's Cube holds an immense significance. Venture with us as we explore the possibilities that lie within the realms of the multiverse and its connection to this sacred symbol.

Metatron's Cube is a symbol that has been revered by spiritual seekers for centuries. Its intricate design holds a multitude of geometrical forms which serve as gateways into the profound mysteries of the universe. It is believed to contain the blueprint of creation, connecting us to the interconnectedness of infinite realities.

The concept of multiple universes can be mind-boggling, but Metatron's Cube provides us a pathway to understanding this complex notion. As we delve deeper into the symbolism of this sacred symbol, we are offered a glimpse into the vastness of the multiverse and the potential for infinite possibilities.

What makes Metatron's Cube truly fascinating is the way it encapsulates the interconnectedness of all things. It represents the harmonious relationship between the spiritual and physical dimensions, creating a bridge between the seen and unseen realms. Through the exploration of this symbol, we are led to question our own existence and our place in the grand tapestry of the universe.

Metatron's Cube invites us to foster a sense of curiosity and openness to the profound mysteries that lie beyond our limited perception. It encourages us to expand our consciousness and explore the spiritual truths that can be found within the symbol's intricacies. This symbol serves as a reminder that we are an integral part of the greater whole, and our journey of self-discovery is intimately intertwined with the exploration of the multiverse.

As we embark on this exploration of the multiverse and Metatron's Cube, we invite you, our diverse audience united by a shared interest in spirituality, metaphysics, symbolism, and personal growth, to join us on this journey. Together, let us delve into the depths of the unknown and uncover the infinite possibilities that await us.

15. The Future of Metatron's Cube

Evolution of Consciousness

Welcome to the subchapter on the evolution of consciousness. In this section, we will explore how Metatron's Cube can potentially impact the evolution of human consciousness and contribute to the collective awakening of individuals.

Metatron's Cube is a powerful symbol that represents the interconnectedness of all things in the universe. It is believed to hold profound spiritual insights and mysteries that can lead to personal growth and transformation.

As we delve into the exploration of the evolution of consciousness, we are invited to approach the subject with reverence, curiosity, and an open mind. The mysteries encapsulated within Metatron's Cube ignite a sense of wonder and awe, prompting us to question the nature of our existence and the possibilities that lie beyond the realms of our current understanding.

The evolution of consciousness is a journey that encompasses the exploration and expansion of our awareness, understanding, and connection to the world around us. Through this process, we are able to transcend the limitations of our ego and tap into a higher state of consciousness that is aligned with the deeper truths of the universe.

Metatron's Cube serves as a catalyst for this transformation by creating a resonance within us that activates dormant potentials and awakens new levels of consciousness. It stimulates our innate curiosity and encourages us to explore the essence of our being, the interplay of patterns and energies, and the interconnected web of existence.

As we delve deeper into the symbolism of Metatron's Cube, we begin to recognize that the evolution of consciousness is not merely an individual endeavor. It is a collective process that involves the awakening of humanity as a whole. The resonance of Metatron's Cube serves as a unifying force, connecting individuals who share a common interest in spirituality, metaphysics, symbolism, and personal growth.

Through the exploration of Metatron's Cube and its potential impact on the evolution of human consciousness, we are invited to embark on a profound journey of self-discovery, expansion, and transformation. It is a journey that holds the promise of unlocking our true potential, unveiling hidden wisdom, and experiencing a deep sense of connection with the divine.

Influence on Human Evolution

The symbol of Metatron's Cube holds profound mysteries and spiritual insights that have the potential to transform our understanding of human consciousness, DNA activation, and spiritual evolution. Its intricate geometry and symbolic representations reveal a deep connection between the physical and spiritual realms.

As we delve into the influence of Metatron's Cube on human evolution, we are invited to embark on a journey of reverence, curiosity, and openness to the transformative power of this sacred symbol. It is through this exploration that we can begin to grasp the profound implications it has for our personal and collective growth.

The geometry of Metatron's Cube is composed of thirteen circles that are interconnected by lines and arches. This intricate pattern reflects the interconnectedness of all things in the universe and serves as a reminder of the sacred geometry that underlies the fabric of existence.

When we contemplate the implications of Metatron's Cube on human evolution, we are confronted with the realization that our journey towards greater self-awareness and spiritual awakening is intricately linked to the secrets encoded within this symbol.

One of the ways in which Metatron's Cube influences human evolution is through its connection to DNA activation. As we explore the sacred geometry of the symbol, we begin to understand that it represents the blueprint of creation itself. Its intricate patterns and interconnectedness evoke a sense of resonance with the fundamental building blocks of life.

Through conscious engagement with Metatron's Cube, we can activate dormant aspects of our DNA, unlocking hidden potentials and accessing higher states of consciousness. This activation process aligns us with the cosmic energies and spiritual forces that permeate the universe, propelling us towards a more expanded and enlightened state of being.

Furthermore, working with Metatron's Cube accelerates not only personal growth but also collective growth. As more individuals embrace this symbol and incorporate its teachings into their lives, a ripple effect is created that contributes to the emergence of a new paradigm of existence.

The profound mysteries and spiritual insights encapsulated within Metatron's Cube serve as a catalyst for global awakening and transformation. It calls upon us to question the limitations of our current belief systems and embrace a more expansive understanding of reality.

In conclusion, the influence of Metatron's Cube on human evolution is vast and multifaceted. Its sacred geometry, DNA activation properties, and transformative power contribute to the evolution of our consciousness, individually and collectively. By exploring the depths of this symbol with reverence, curiosity, and an open mind, we can tap into the profound mysteries and spiritual insights that it holds, and ultimately accelerate our personal and collective growth.

Metatron's Cube in the New Era

Metatron's Cube in the New Era

When we contemplate the role of Metatron's Cube in the new era, we are invited to explore the profound mysteries and spiritual insights encapsulated within this sacred symbol. With a sense of reverence and curiosity, we open ourselves up to the transformative power it holds.

Metatron's Cube, an intricate geometric pattern composed of interconnected spheres, emanates an energy that resonates deeply with those who are drawn to spirituality, metaphysics, symbolism, and personal growth. It has the ability to awaken dormant aspects of our consciousness and guide us on a journey of self-discovery and expansion.

In this new era of spiritual awakening, Metatron's Cube serves as a powerful catalyst for conscious living and global transformation. Its sacred geometry represents the unity and interconnectedness of all aspects of existence. Through its balanced and harmonious structure, it reflects the inherent order and divine intelligence of the universe.

As we delve deeper into the symbolism of Metatron's Cube, we begin to realize its potential implications for shaping the future of humanity. By contemplating and meditating on this sacred symbol, we can tap into higher levels of consciousness and unlock hidden potentials within ourselves.

Metatron's Cube reminds us that we are not separate from the divine, but an integral part of it. It invites us to embrace our spiritual essence and align ourselves with the higher purpose of our existence. Through this alignment, we can contribute to the collective evolution of humanity and create a more conscious and harmonious world.

As we embark on this journey of exploration and transformation, let us approach the symbol of Metatron's Cube with an open mind and heart. Let us allow its energy to guide us towards a deeper understanding of ourselves and the interconnected web of existence. In doing so, we can truly embrace the power of Metatron's Cube in the new era and actively participate in the global awakening and conscious evolution that is unfolding before us.

Also by M.A Hill

Minimalist Living How to Become a Minimalist
Minimalism How to Live a Happier Life by Becoming a Minimalist
The Magic of Auras How to See, Feel and Heal the Human Auras
Wiccan Candle Spells and Candle Magick
Clear seeing and the sixth sense: The brow Chakra: The Guide on How to Awaken the Amazing Power you Already Have and Go Beyond the Physical Eyes
Root Chakra The Powerful Kundalini Energy
The 7 Chakras: Balancing, Colors and Meaning
Switching to a Vegan Lifestyle
Essential Oils for Natural Living
Unlocking the Secrets of the Universe: A Journey through the Sacred Geometry
"The Enchanted Realms: The Existence and Origins of Fairies."
Vanished Without a Trace: Unsolved Mysteries that Haunt Us Today
Unlocking the Flame: A Journey into Candle Magic
From Archangel to Geometry: Metatron's Cube and Its Spiritual Legacy